THE WATER CRISIS

UNDERSTANDING GLOBAL ISSUES

Published by Smart Apple Media
1980 Lookout Drive
North Mankato, Minnesota 56003
USA

This book is based on *The Water Crisis: A Matter of Life and Death*
Copyright © 2001 Understanding Global Issues Ltd., Cheltenham, England

Library of Congress Cataloging-in-Publication Data

The water crisis / edited by Jared Keen.
    p. cm.—(Understanding global issues)
Includes index.
Summary: Examines the environmental, social, and economic issues involved in the use
of freshwater around the world.
  ISBN 1-58340-172-5 (hardcover: alk. paper)
 1. Water-supply—Juvenile literature. [1. Water supply.] I. Keen,
Jared. II. Series.
 TD348 .W373 2002
 363.6'1—dc21

                    2001008449

Printed in Malaysia
2 4 6 8 9 7 5 3 1

EDITOR Jared Keen   **COPY EDITOR** Jennifer Nault
PHOTO RESEARCHER Gayle Murdoff   **DESIGNER** Terry Paulhus

Contents

Introduction

Seventy-one percent of the surface of Earth is covered by water. Most of this is seawater. In fact, less than one percent of the water on Earth is freshwater. Of this, only half is usable. More importantly, freshwater resources are not evenly distributed. Canada, for example, has one-fifth of the world's freshwater. Most countries do not have enough water to cover their needs.

It is hard to believe, but there is not enough water in the world to meet our needs, and much of what we use is wasted. Most of the rivers and lakes in the world are polluted. Many species of the plants and animals that live in rivers and lakes are in danger of extinction. The world's farmers are wasting so much water that they are creating deserts where there used to be freshwater. The World Water Council says that by the year 2025, most of the world will suffer from severe water shortages unless we do what we can right now to save the water we have.

The difference between the rich and the poor is clear in the amount of water that people use. Some people in the world use barely 2.2 gallons (10 L) of water per day, while others use more

Billions of people worldwide are without access to clean drinking water.

than 110 gallons (500 L) of water per day. Twenty percent of people in the world do not have clean water to use for drinking, cooking, or bathing. Two out of five people in the world live in unsanitary conditions. They do not have toilets or sewers to remove their waste.

There is not enough water in the world to cover our needs.

Some parts of the world have plenty of water, while other parts have very little. Moving water from one place to another is difficult and expensive. People in the Middle East, for example, have very severe water shortages because they do not have much water to begin with, and because their population is growing. Wars and other problems also interfere with the water supply.

Other parts of the world depend on monsoons for their water. A monsoon is a seasonal wind that can result in very heavy rainfall during the wet season. Unfortunately, monsoons do not always come every year, and when they do, sometimes there is so much rain that it causes flooding. In fact, there

are 5 times as many flooding disasters in the world now than there were in the 1960s, and the financial cost is 37 times as great. Many of these disasters occur because people have chopped down forests, drained swamps, redirected rivers, or built cities where flooding happens every year.

During the last 100 years, the world's population has more than tripled. Freshwater use has increased sixfold. Planning for future water supply is complicated by uncertainty about climate change and the possibility of northward-shifting patterns of rainfall—which would make water scarcity in many **arid**, or dry, regions even worse than it is today.

FRESHWATER SUPPLIES

Countries with the largest freshwater supplies:

1. Brazil
2. Russia
3. Canada
4. China
5. Indonesia
6. United States
7. Bangladesh
8. India
9. Myanmar
10. Democratic Republic of Congo

A Civilizing Influence

Two thousand years ago, Rome's water system supplied drinking water to houses, filled an extensive array of public and private baths, and carried away sewage. Although today's water engineers have access to far more sophisticated technology, billions of people in dozens of countries worldwide still have neither piped drinking water nor sanitation services.

The beginnings of large-scale irrigation probably date back at least 7,000 years to the Egyptians, who brought water to their fields from the Nile River. Mesopotamian civilization

---

Aqueducts became a symbol of the power of the Roman Empire.

(fourth millennium B.C.) was based on irrigation developed in the fertile land between the Tigris and Euphrates Rivers. Among the pioneers in this region were the Sumerians. Later, King Nebuchadnezzar II (605–562 B.C.) developed Babylon into a major city, which, even at that time, had reliable drinking water and efficient sewers.

Aqueducts became a symbol of the power and technology of the Roman Empire, with pipelines on aqueducts bringing water to about 100 cities in Africa, Asia Minor, and Europe.

Aqueducts are artificial channels for carrying water. Roman aqueducts generally took the form of a bridge. By the 4th century A.D., in the reign of the Roman Emperor Constantine, 19 water pipelines, covering a total distance of 270 miles (436 km), converged on Rome. Responsibility for the water supplies lay with the water director and his 700 technicians, who had to distribute 260 million gallons (984 million L) of water per day. The water flowing from the various pipelines was stored in Rome in water tanks with a fairly low capacity—the system was designed to be dispersed rapidly.

Any water left over was used to clean the city and the sewers. This knowledge was lost after the fall of the Roman Empire in the fifth century. Water management and sanitation remained at primitive levels throughout the Middle Ages. Indeed, much of Europe remained without piped water or sanitation until the 20th century.

Roman water engineering depended entirely on gravity. It was not until after the **Industrial Revolution** began in the late 18th century that it became possible, with the aid of pumping systems, to transport water uphill. The technology of steam-driven pumps and the scientific discovery of a link between dirty water and disease made water engineering as important a profession as it had been during the days of the Roman Empire. Many common diseases were virtually eradicated in Europe, and the life expectancy and general health of the population improved dramatically as clean water and sewage systems were made widely available.

Today, billions of people worldwide still lack clean drinking water and basic sanitation. The knowledge exists to provide these basics to every person on the planet, but the political will to do so is weak. Meanwhile, we waste water by using more of it than we need, by polluting the water we have, and through wasteful farming

■ **The first Roman aqueduct was constructed in 312 B.C.**

methods. Irrigation consumes two-thirds of all the freshwater used by humans and helps provide 40 percent of the world's food. Irrigation tends to be a very wasteful method of farming, though, especially when **intensive** farming methods are used. In addition, irrigation often damages the land. Salt water is ruining more than 2.5 millions acres (1 million h) of land each year, while the runoff from chemicals used in farming is contaminating many underground water supplies. If future generations are to have enough food and water to **sustain** themselves, farming practices must be modified to include better water conservation and management practices.

Even diet has an impact on the water supply. The production of 1 ton (0.9 t) of chicken meat takes twice as much water as 1 ton (0.9 t) of rice, while beef production uses 10 times as much water. Thus, the trend toward meat-eating in the **developing world**—a sign of economic improvement—

A Civilizing Influence

is putting an extra strain on water resources.

Rice is a major food source in Asia, but its cultivation uses a large amount of water, adding to problems of water scarcity in China, India, Pakistan, and Bangladesh. Many farmers have resorted to using power-driven wells to raise underground water for irrigation. Water tables are dropping as rates of consumption exceed the rate at which aquifers are replenished. Aquifers are natural underground storage systems made of rock, through which water flows and in which water is stored. Aquifers have been used for thousands of years, but water is so scarce in some regions that it is hard to see how traditional forms of agriculture can be sustained.

MESOPOTAMIAN IRRIGATION PRACTICES

Early civilization began in Mesopotamia, a region that included what is now Iraq and part of Iran. Mesopotamians relied heavily on irrigation because soil in the region was of poor quality and rainfall was scarce. The Tigris and Euphrates Rivers provided water that could be diverted to irrigate Mesopotamian fields. In order to do this, a system of canals was dug. The canal system required constant maintenance because silt would accumulate quickly, blocking the flow of irrigation water. Flooding was also a problem. **Salinization** could not be overcome by the technology of the time. As a result, the same practices that allowed agriculture to flourish in the area ultimately made the fields too salinized to be used.

Egyptians have been measuring the water levels of the Nile River for 5,000 years.

Rice cultivation originated in China nearly 10,000 years ago. Ancient irrigation systems are still in use.

KEY CONCEPTS

Irrigation Irrigation is the practice of moving water from a river or storage area across land. Some areas that receive insufficient amounts of rainfall are irrigated to grow crops. Irrigation has been practiced for thousands of years around the world.

Industrial Revolution The Industrial Revolution began in Great Britain in the 18th century. Rapid technological advancements changed the way industrial processes were carried out. Modernization spread throughout Europe and North America in the 1800s, sparking a shift from rural to urban living. Factories began to replace workshops, and machines took the place of handwork. The Industrial Revolution marked a major turning point for business and industry.

Freshwater Resources

In the past century, the world's population has more than tripled. At the same time, our water consumption is 6 times what it was 100 years ago. Yet, we have far less freshwater available to us now—much of the supply is polluted.

There appears to be so much water in the world. How could we ever run out? This seems to be a valid question, but in truth, less than one percent of the world's total water is freshwater—suitable for drinking, farming, or industry. Still, that leaves more than 1.9 million gallons (7.2 million L) of freshwater a year for every human being on Earth. All of the plants and animals on Earth need freshwater, too. If human beings used all of that water for themselves, the forests and farms would dry up, and the animals would die. In addition, not all freshwater is of the highest quality, nor is it evenly distributed across the planet.

Some countries have more than 5.2 million gallons (19.6 million L) of freshwater per person, while others have less than 52,000 gallons (200,000 L) per person. In many of the world's poorest countries, where freshwater is most scarce, the population is growing so quickly that the amount of freshwater available to each person is diminishing daily.

Where does our freshwater come from? Freshwater falls as rain, snow, or hail. Evaporation and plant **transpiration** cause water vapor to rise into the air, where it condenses into clouds.

Desalinated water is far too expensive for widespread use in farming.

When precipitation in the form of rain, hail, or snow reaches land, it flows toward the sea in rivers or soaks into the soil as groundwater—which also flows toward the sea, unless it becomes trapped in rock or aquifers. The more runoff there is from precipitation, the more water there is available for human use. Runoff varies greatly from continent to continent. Asia has 30 percent of the world's runoff, whereas Africa has only 10 percent. Runoff is sometimes called "blue water," as distinct from the "green water" stored in soil and taken up by plants.

If the salt could be removed cheaply and easily from seawater, so that it could be used in households, factories, and on farmland, the world's water problems would be solved. In fact, many industries in the Middle East and California already use what is called desalinated water—seawater that has had the salt removed. Some countries, such as Saudi Arabia,

■ **Nearly 150,000 gallons (660,000 L) of freshwater flow over Niagara Falls every second.**

have invested large amounts of money in desalination plants. Saudi Arabia has almost twice as much desalination capacity as the United States. The oil-rich Arab countries have more desalination capacity than the rest of the world put together. Unfortunately, the desalination process requires a large amount of energy and is very expensive. It also generates salt waste, and desalination plants are left with the problem of what to do with all of the salt removed from the water. Desalinated water is still far too expensive for widespread use in farming, which is where the world uses most of its water. In 2000, desalination supplied about 0.2 percent of the world's freshwater. This percentage is unlikely to change much in the foreseeable future unless a cheap new energy source becomes widely available.

Many countries are finding water today in places where it will not be available for much longer. Libya, for example, pumps water from ancient aquifers far beneath the ground. At the rate Libya is using this source of water, the aquifers will be empty in 50 to 100 years. Saudi Arabia grows wheat in desert conditions by irrigating the crops with underground aquifers. These aquifers will never be refilled with water because there is virtually no rain in Saudi Arabia. The aquifers will be empty within 50 years, and then the wheat fields will dry up within the course of a few weeks. The story is the same all over the world: from the Middle East to China, from the United States to Africa, the world's aquifers are being drained of million-year-old supplies of freshwater. About 40 percent of the world's population in 80 countries is already experiencing severe water shortages.

Water cannot be created, so it has to be shared. Earth's supply of water is the same now as it was one million years ago. Unfortunately, there are many more people in the world and many freshwater resources have been so damaged by pollution that the total supply of water is diminishing before we even have the chance to use it. Unlike food, fuel, minerals, or manufactured goods, water cannot easily be transported from one part of the globe to another. The quantities needed for farming—the main consumer of water—are simply too large.

Major dams, pipelines, and aqueduct systems can store great volumes of water and transfer it hundreds of miles. However, these facilities are very costly and often have a negative impact on the environment. In addition, these projects only fix regional problems. They have little or no affect on global water shortages.

Even a rich country such as the United States, with access to the latest technology, cannot rule out a water crisis in the

OGALLALA AQUIFER

This natural underground reservoir covers 320,000 square miles (830,000 sq km) and is located beneath the Great Plains of the U.S. It is the largest and most heavily developed aquifer in the world. Water from the aquifer is being used at a high rate for irrigation and residential services. There is concern that the water supply is being used faster than it can be replenished.

█████ **Saudi Arabia uses about 40 percent of all the desalinated water produced in the Middle East.**

Livestock production accounts for nearly half of all the water consumed in the United States.

future. Half of the rivers and lakes in the U.S. have been damaged by pollution. Some public waterworks have had to shut down because of groundwater pollution. The most serious problems are in the arid southwestern states, such as California, Arizona, and New Mexico, where the amount of water being used is greater than the amount of water the region can bring in to replace it. Southern California is, after all, a desert, and yet the area is densely populated and is well known for its golf courses, lush gardens, swimming pools, and huge farming operations. The massive amounts of water

---

The amount of water pumped out of the ground has become a problem.

---

required to sustain the Southern California lifestyle do not occur naturally in the region. California's Central Valley is one of the top farming areas in the United States only because of the large amount of water transported to the region via huge water pipelines. The high cost of this water is paid for by the taxpayer.

The amount of water pumped out of the ground has become a serious problem. One-third of the water used for irrigation in the United States comes from aquifers beneath the Great Plains between South Dakota and northwest Texas. The massive Ogallala aquifer has

KEY CONCEPTS

Desalination The process of removing salt from seawater provides limited amounts of water for drinking and irrigation. Desalination is receiving increasing attention, but the process is far too expensive to be effective on a global scale.

Runoff After precipitation falls to Earth, it begins to move in accordance with the laws of gravity. Some precipitation is absorbed by the ground, but most of it flows downhill as runoff. Runoff amounts are affected by several factors,

including soil type, elevation, slope, and vegetation. Runoff from cultivated land often carries excess nutrients, which can ultimately degrade water quality.

been overpumped to the point where at least one-quarter of the reserve has been depleted. In Texas, cattle ranchers and other farmers do not know whether they will be able to continue ranching—beef production requires large amounts of water, and the future of the water supply in the area is uncertain. Also, the cost of pumping has increased because wells have to be dug deeper and deeper to reach the water. Eventually, the wells will be so deep that the water will be too salty to be used.

Canada contains about one-fifth of the world's freshwater. This is in contrast to the U.S., which is experiencing water shortages in many areas. In the 1960s, American engineers devised fanciful schemes to divert some of Canada's major rivers southward. In the 21st century, plans to ship water from Canada were being revived. In 2001, a Canadian businessman proposed to pay $12.8 million per month to take 13 billion gallons (59 billion L) of water each year from a Newfoundland lake and ship it to the United States. However, the federal government in Canada is pushing its provinces and territories to agree to a national ban on the bulk removal of water from all drainage basins. In 2001, Canadian Trade Minister Pierre Pettigrew stated that "water is not a [tradable] good, it is a resource that needs to be managed." In the short term, it seems unlikely that the U.S. will solve its water shortage by shipping water from Canada.

Growing cities require more and more water to sustain the numbers of people living there. Some fast-growing cities have been forced to import water or to pump more water from underground aquifers than

nature is able to replace. Water tables are dropping very quickly in Beijing, Bangkok, Mexico City, and other major population centers around the world.

More than five million people die every year due to unsafe drinking water and poor sanitation.

Duties: Analyze information about water resources
Education: Bachelor of science degree
Interests: Water resource management

Navigate to the Environmental Careers Web site: www.eco.org for information on related careers. Also click on www.environmental-jobs.com for more information about hydrology jobs.

Careers in Focus

A hydrologist analyzes information about water resources in specific areas. These areas are called watersheds, and they can contain rivers, streams, lakes, or other large bodies of water.

A hydrologist's day-to-day duties include managing staff, developing budgets, and designing programs to develop or protect a watershed. He or she may also produce reports about the environmental impact of developments within watersheds.

Typically, a hydrologist's time is divided between laboratory work and field work. Hydrologists often travel to watersheds to collect water samples, which they then inspect in a laboratory to determine water quality. If the water quality in a watershed is low, a hydrologist will make recommendations about how to improve the quality.

Hydrologists may specialize in surface-water hydrology (the study of streams, lakes, and **estuaries**), groundwater hydrology, or hydrogeology (the study of sub-surface water).

Hydrogeologists are concerned with the occurrence, circulation, and distribution of water flowing through the ground. They study the quality and quantity of this groundwater. Hydrogeologists often work in the field. Back in the office, they use maps, records, models, and reports to do their job. A degree in geology or a related environmental subject is required.

Engineering Solutions

In the past century, whenever humans have been faced with water shortages, they have sought engineering solutions. They have built dams, diverted rivers, built canals, or invested in other major projects to manage water. More than 40,000 large dams have been built worldwide, and many more are under construction or are planned. Dams enable water to be regulated. This reduces the risk of floods and harnesses the water for irrigation or power generation. Still, large dams can have a catastrophic effect on the environment and on the people living near them.

More than 40,000 large dams have been built worldwide.

Fewer big dams are being built today. Since 1980, about 500 dams have been removed in the United States. However, major cities use large amounts of water and often need to build large dams and reservoirs to meet this need. In rural areas, small dams, built by local communities, have an important role to play in improving the management of water resources.

The Tennessee Valley Authority in the U.S., the Grande Dixence system in Switzerland, and the diversion of the Amu Darya and the Syr Darya Rivers in Russia are just a few of the

major projects completed during the past 100 years. India's ongoing Narmada Valley project involves building 30 large dams and hundreds of smaller ones. When the project is finished, the water will irrigate five million acres (2 million h) of land and deliver drinking water to approximately 8,000 villages. Turkey plans to build numerous dams and various irrigation systems and hydroelectric power plants in the southeast part of the country. China's Three Gorges project will divert water from the Yangtze River to the North China Plain in addition to creating a series of massive dams, which are intended to control annual flooding and provide hydroelectric power.

While all of these projects sound as though they will bring great benefits to the people who live in these regions, there are huge human and environmental costs involved in projects of this scale. For example, when the Erie Canal was built in New York State, the sea lamprey was unintentionally introduced to the Great Lakes, killing most of the Great Lakes species of salmon and ruining the fishing industry there. The diversion of the Amu Darya and the Syr Darya Rivers in Russia made the Aral Sea dry up to the point that it killed all the fish. The Aral Sea was, at one time, the fourth-largest body of freshwater in the world. The completion of the Aswan Dam in Egypt reduced the amount of fertile sediment in the irrigation water, forcing Egyptian farmers to use large amounts of chemical fertilizers. In China, the Three Gorges project will force more than one million people to move. In India, current dam construction projects will displace more than 700,000 people. In many parts of the world, plant and animal species are endangered because their habitats have been altered by water management projects.

One of the world's most ambitious water engineering

Water is a major source of renewable energy. Dams can harness the power of moving water to produce electricity.

projects is the Great Man-made River in Libya. This $32 billion project pumps water from ancient aquifers 1,640 feet (500 m) beneath the southern desert. The water is then carried in huge pipelines to the northern coastal zones 1,180 miles (1,900 km) away, where it is used for agricultural, industrial, and domestic purposes. Unfortunately, the project will provide only temporary relief. The ancient aquifers could be exhausted within 50 years, leaving desalination

of Mediterranean seawater as Libya's only hope for a stable supply of freshwater.

The Rhine River flows through the center of Europe. It is one of the world's most engineered rivers. One authority described the Rhine as "no longer really a river but an engineered waterway of **levees**, concrete embankments, locks, flow-control devices, hydro plants, weirs, and channels." The Rhine supplies numerous cities, towns, and factories in Germany, Austria, the Czech Republic, and Slovakia with freshwater, but the river is too polluted for any fish or birds to live in it. The river's flood plains have been developed into cities and towns, and the river itself is little more than a convenient sewer. Businesses up and down the river dump toxic chemicals and other waste into it. Efforts have been made to clean up the Rhine and other European rivers, such as the Danube, but the cost is great, and it requires the cooperation of numerous governments.

In the 1960s, more than 350 large dams (dams over 49 feet or

Many of Europe's rivers have been extensively engineered.

Municipal water treatment plants must meet stringent standards to ensure that wastewater has been properly treated.

15 m high) were built every year worldwide. As the 21st century begins, the annual total has fallen to about 150. In the United States, there is a growing movement to demolish existing dams that require heavy maintenance or damage the environment. Governments everywhere are finally beginning to understand that the environment needs to be taken into account when planning new water engineering projects. Russia appears to have abandoned the plan to **divert** Siberian rivers southward to bring water into arid regions of central Asia. Now, water managers are assessing the need to protect the number of plant and animal species that depend on freshwater for their survival.

Dams are necessary for water management. They provide storage and distribution facilities in areas where rainfall is inconsistent or seasonal. The ideal dam is built where there are large amounts of precipitation, where steep hills catch the water quickly, and where the soil is hard enough that water is not lost to ground absorption. Evaporation is not as great a problem in mountainous or hilly areas, but some evaporation from the surface of the collected water will occur. Engineers today calculate the **optimal** size of a reservoir based on local evaporation rates. The Aswan Dam in southern Egypt loses a large amount of water to evaporation because of its location. The mountains of Ethiopia would provide a better location for a dam, but Egypt is wary of permitting another country to have power over its water supply.

Many dams are broadly-based earth embankments with layers of materials, some very **porous** and some not. This provides stability to the structure. Such dams are usually built from whatever rock is most easily accessible in the region. Masonry or concrete dams are supported by arches or buttresses

KEY CONCEPTS

Water management When faced with water shortages, people in the last century solved the problem by building dams, reservoirs, canals, and other major water management facilities. Unfortunately, these large projects often hurt the environment or the people they were intended to help. Many thousands of people have been forced to move because a dam flooded the area where they live. Dams are necessary for managing water where rain is seasonal or for large populations. Still, there are ways and places to build dams that are more efficient than others are.

Water purification Water can be purified via several chemical treatments. Chlorine has been used since it was discovered in Sweden in 1774. Iodine is another common disinfectant and has been used to purify water for nearly 100 years. It is safe for short-term use (three to six months), but long-term consumption is not recommended. Filtration is an effective method of water purification, too, when coupled with chemical treatment.

The Hoover Dam has the capacity to meet the energy needs of nearly one million people.

to give them extra strength. Giant dams that drown valleys and cause environmental havoc (such as preventing the breeding and **migration** of fish) may do more harm than good. The question is how to design water management projects that cause little or no disturbance to people or the environment. Essentially, this means shifting toward smaller-scale projects in which local communities can be directly involved. For cities, however, this approach may be impractical—large dams may be unavoidable. Towns depend on service water stored in reservoirs and piped to end users. Before such water can be used, even for industrial processes, it has to undergo a costly treatment process. Water purification plants remove bacteria and chemical **pollutants** from the water. Some can even reclaim wastewater from the sewers and recycle it back to consumers as drinking water.

Duties: Design dams and supervise construction
Education: Bachelor of engineering degree
Interests: Construction, math, drawing, and physics

Navigate to the Environmental Careers Web site: www.eco.org for information on related careers. Also click on www.engineeringjobs.com for more information about jobs involving engineering.

Careers in Focus

Hydraulics engineers are in charge of designing dams. They often organize and supervise the construction, too.

Hydraulics engineers need to have strong math, drawing, and computer skills. They must also be familiar with building materials, environmental issues, and safety regulations. Analytical and problem-solving abilities should complement a keen eye for detail.

Most of the time, hydraulics engineers work in an office environment, where they use computer-aided design (CAD) systems to develop plans for the structure they are building. Occasionally, hydraulics engineers must visit job sites. When hydraulics engineers are conducting fieldwork, the conditions are often stressful. Surveying proposed dam sites may require travel to isolated areas, walking long distances on rocky terrain, working in confined spaces, and climbing to significant heights.

In order to succeed at their jobs, hydraulics engineers must be skilled communicators, both written and verbal. Proposing projects requires consultation with a variety of agencies, organizations, and professionals.

Irrigation Old and New

Irrigation is popular because farmers can grow much more through this method of farming than any other. Worldwide, 670 million acres (270 million h) of farmland are irrigated, with irrigated farms in Asia accounting for 70 percent of the total. The amount of irrigated land has doubled since 1960, increasing the amount of food produced in the world. Today, the growth in population is greater than the growth in the use of irrigated land, meaning that the

Traditional labor-intensive irrigation systems are still common in developing countries.

current total food supply, relative to the population it is intended to feed, is shrinking.

Most irrigation methods are very inefficient in terms of water use.

Irrigated cropland is usually much more productive than land that depends on rainfall alone. Unfortunately, most irrigation methods are very inefficient in terms of water use. Since irrigated farming accounts for 70 percent of annual water

consumption worldwide (and more than 90 percent in some countries, such as India), a relatively small improvement in efficiency would make a big difference to the amount of water used.

Irrigation is the practice of channeling water from a river or storage area across a large expanse of land. The water is usually stored in dams and reservoirs. While some of the stored water comes from rivers, the rest comes from rain. It is necessary to store the water because, in some parts of the world, it rains for only a few months of the year, and the rest

of the year is dry. As humans, animals, and plants need water year-round, storing the water makes it available for more than just the few months that it rains. Irrigation is a very productive method of farming. About 40 percent of the world's food comes from the 18 percent of the world's farms that are irrigated.

The problem with irrigation is that it can be bad for the environment. Sometimes, large farms pump too deeply from the underground aquifers and end up irrigating with salt water. Unfortunately, saltwater contamination, or salinization, can destroy large areas of otherwise fertile farmland for thousands of years. Also, even farms that use freshwater for irrigation waste much of the water through evaporation and by watering the land in a way that does not reach the roots of the crops. If farmers saved more water when they irrigated, the

world would not be faced with such water shortages.

Early irrigation methods ranged from the simple use of hand-held buckets to elaborate systems of canals, terraces, and water wheels. Irrigation systems were used in the Inca and Aztec Empires (13th to mid-16th century) and by previous civilizations in the New World. Some of these early societies collapsed, though, because poor irrigation practices ruined the land through salinization. This

Modern irrigation practices, such as this sprinkler, rely on automated systems.

is believed to be the reason Mesopotamian civilization died out. Worldwide, similar problems now affect more than 2.5 million acres (1 million h) of additional land every year.

The science of irrigation probably spread from Babylon to ancient China, which had the technology by around 2000 B.C. One of China's best-known

TOP FIVE IRRIGATORS

For every 100 gallons (450 L) of water used in the world, 70 gallons (315 L) irrigate farmland.

In terms of area, these countries irrigate the most land:
1. China—128 million acres (52 million h)
2. Thailand—12.4 million acres (5 million h)
3. Indonesia—11.8 million acres (4.8 million h)
4. Japan—6.6 million acres (2.7 million h)
5. Vietnam—5.7 million acres (2.3 million h)

structures is the 1,114-mile (1,795-km) Grand Canal linking North and South China. It is the world's oldest and longest canal. Construction began in 486 B.C. The canal is still in use today. The Chinese government is linking this ancient structure to the massive new Yangtze diversion scheme.

Another early large-scale project in China supplied irrigation water to the Red Basin in the province of Sichuan. The River Min was split into two arms, from which 520 large canals branched off, feeding countless smaller ones. This irrigation network has been continuously maintained since its creation. Nearly 70 percent of China's food production depends on irrigation. In the developing world as a whole, about 60 percent of rice and 40 percent of wheat come from irrigated land.

In the ancient Middle East, irrigation was carried out by an entirely different method of engineering. Unlike Asia, where irrigation carried water on surface canals, irrigation in the Middle East was carried out via underground canals that tapped groundwater. A main well would be sunk below the water table in an upland area, and the water would then be brought to farmland or towns by means of gently sloping canals—traveling largely underground. These systems were called "foggara" in North Africa and Arabia and "qanats" in Asia Minor. The advantage of this method of

irrigation is that it permitted early civilizations to develop without dependence on rainfall. There were 40,000 qanats in Iran alone, and many of them were still in use in the 1970s.

Sixty percent of the water in irrigation channels is lost to evaporation or seepage.

Another advantage of the qanat system was that it tapped groundwater without using pumps—the aquifer would never be depleted beyond its natural state. However, qanats required continuous maintenance, a large labor force, and a high level of organization. Modern mechanical pumps have made access to groundwater easier, and now, few farmers rely on the old qanat method of irrigation. Also, since a large portion of the population has moved from the countryside to the towns— where jobs are more plentiful and better paid—the traditional water engineering skills have been lost.

Worldwide, the most common method of irrigation is still the ancient one of open channels, which water crop areas by simple gravity. This system is inexpensive, but 60 percent of the water is lost to evaporation

▬ **Excessive salinization can turn once-fertile soil into barren land.**

or seepage before reaching the crop roots. Two other forms of irrigation involve complete **inundation** or overhead sprinkling. Micro-irrigation is one of the latest developments in crop cultivation. Small amounts of water "drip" directly into the ground near the plant's roots from a perforated pipe lying on or beneath the surface. One advantage of this method is that the roots are permanently wet, which prevents salt from building up around the roots—a

common problem of irrigation. The drip method is now used on well over half of the irrigated land in Israel.

In some arid areas, such as the Namib Desert, water is collected from the condensation, or heavy dew, that occurs when daytime and nighttime temperatures vary widely. Properly managed, this dew can provide enough moisture to grow plants. Fog is also collected in some parts of the world, for example in Chile, Peru, Ecuador, and Oman. Huge nets are placed on hillsides. Fog condenses on the mesh and then drips into collection troughs, providing water for local communities that would otherwise have too little to survive.

Farmers have long been aware of the dangers of irrigation. Unless irrigation is properly managed, the soil can become waterlogged if too much water is used, or salty if the soil is not properly drained. If crops are waterlogged, the plant roots become oversaturated and die from lack of oxygen. Alternatively, if the natural salts collected by water as it flows downhill are allowed to concentrate around the roots, the crops will not grow. Among agricultural researchers, the race is on to develop salt-resistant crops.

The problem of salt in the soil is common in hot climates. Large areas of land have been turned into useless salt flats. Every year, 2.5–3.7 million acres

KEY CONCEPTS

Salinization All irrigation water contains small quantities of salt. When surface water evaporates, this salt is left behind. The quantities of salt are usually too small to be of concern, but salt can accumulate, eventually becoming toxic to plants. Areas that receive little rainfall are more prone to salinization than areas that receive significant amounts of rainfall—rain washes away salt. Salinization is most problematic in desert areas, such as Africa, but it also poses a threat to U.S. farmers. Salinization affects 25–30 percent of land irrigated in the U.S.

A single, simple pump, such as this one in Ethiopia, is often used by entire communities to obtain water.

(1–1.5 million h) of farmland are damaged by salt or waterlogging. Egypt and Pakistan are losing 30 percent of their potential harvests because of this. Thorough research into the causes of salt build-up has been conducted only in recent years. Even in the United States, where agricultural science is highly developed, one-quarter of irrigated land has been damaged by salt build-up.

Major irrigation projects are becoming more expensive because the most suitable land and water sources have already been used. New projects in India, China, Indonesia, and Pakistan may cost $600–$1,600 per acre ($1,500–$4,000 per h) for the necessary dams and water distribution systems. In Africa, the cost can be as high as $8,000 per acre ($20,000 per h) because of small crop areas and lack of **infrastructure**. Still, even low-tech irrigation can greatly increase the efficiency of water use. Simple techniques include the lining of irrigation channels (so that water does not seep into the ground) and the use of "surge" irrigation (where water is released in two stages, the first helping to seal the soil, the second to irrigate crops).

The choice of crop has an important bearing on water use. Sugar cane, for example, needs 10 times as much water as potatoes do and 30 times as much as pearl millet does. Pearl millet is a grain that ripens very quickly—usually in 60 to 80 days—and is a staple food in many developing countries. Unfortunately, farmers are not motivated to select crops that use low amounts of water because governments pay most of the water costs. In terms of water use, livestock production is less efficient than grain production. Two pounds (1 kg) of beef, for example, may take hundreds of gallons (thousands of liters) of water to produce.

While the best irrigation technology is now very sophisticated and efficient, it is used in relatively few regions. The training of small-scale farmers worldwide is a daunting but essential task that would educate farmers to replace wasteful and damaging irrigation practices with more efficient methods.

Duties: Design and implement systems for sustainable irrigation practices

Education: A diploma in irrigation technology or a degree in agricultural science or engineering

Interests: Efficient water delivery systems

Navigate to the Environmental Careers Web site: www.eco.org for information on related careers. Also click on www.environmental-jobs.com for more information about irrigation jobs.

Careers in Focus

An irrigation technologist has a wide range of duties and responsibilities. He or she is in charge of developing systems for the distribution of water. Some irrigation technologists may specialize in agricultural irrigation, while others may be experts in urban industrial irrigation. Regardless of their area of expertise, irrigation technologists all work toward a common goal: sustainable irrigation strategies and practices.

An irrigation technologist often combines field exploration with office work. He or she will examine aerial photographs, maps, and technical data to assess the irrigation needs of a particular area. Computer-assisted drafting (CAD) programs help irrigation technologists design systems of pumps and pipelines.

Irrigation technologists often have diverse educational backgrounds. Some may have engineering degrees, while others may have agricultural or environmental science backgrounds. Solid math skills are needed to succeed in this field.

Senior irrigation technologists are often responsible for providing information to corporations or private individuals. Strong communication skills, both written and verbal, are necessary to deliver information in a clear and effective manner.

Mapping Water Resources

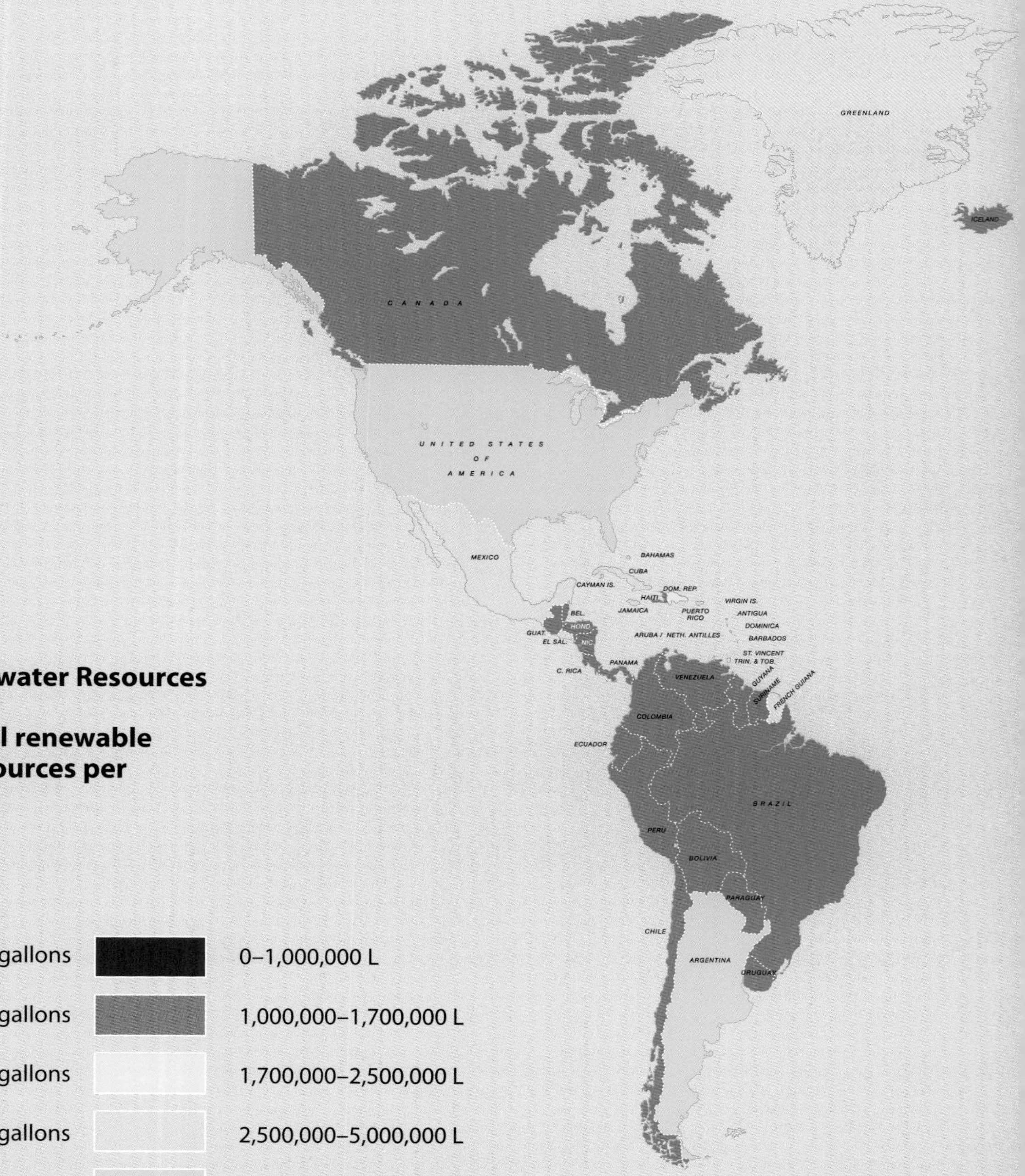

Figure 1: Freshwater Resources

Average annual renewable freshwater resources per capita per year

0–265,000 gallons	0–1,000,000 L
265,000–450,000 gallons	1,000,000–1,700,000 L
450,000–660,000 gallons	1,700,000–2,500,000 L
660,000–1,320,000 gallons	2,500,000–5,000,000 L
1,320,000–2,650,000 gallons	5,000,000–10,000,000 L
More than 2,650,000 gallons	More than 10,000,000 L

NORWAY
SWEDEN
FINLAND

RUSSIAN FEDERATION

IRELAND UK
DEN.
EST.
LATVIA
LITH.
BELARUS

NET.
GERMANY
POLAND

BEL.
LUX.
CZECH
REP.
SLOVAK
REP.
UKRAINE

FRANCE
SWITZ.
AUS.
SLOV.
ROM.

CRO.
BOS.
HERZ.
YUG.
BULG.

ITALY
ALB. MAC.

SPAIN
GREECE
TURKEY
GEORGIA

ARM. AZER.

KAZAKHSTAN

MONGOLIA

GIBRALTAR
MALTA
CYPRUS
LEBANON
SYRIA
IRAQ

KYRGYZSTAN

TAJIKISTAN

N. KOREA
S. KOREA
JAPAN

MOROCCO
ISRAEL

IRAN

CHINA

ARY IS.

WESTERN
SAHARA

ALGERIA

QATAR

NEPAL
BHUTAN

TAIWAN

Hong Kong

MAURITANIA

MALI

CHAD
SUDAN

DJI.

INDIA

MYANMAR
LAOS

ENEGAL
AMBIA
-BISSAU
GUINEA

B. FASO
NIGERIA

ERITREA

ETHIOPIA

SRI
LANKA

THAILAND

VIETNAM

CAMBODIA

PHILIPPINES

S. LEONE
LIBERIA

GHANA
TOGO
BENIN
C.A.R.

SOMALIA

EQ.
GUINEA
CAM.

UGANDA
SOMALIA

MALAYSIA

BRUNEI

GABON
CONGO
Dem. Rep.
CONGO
(former Zaire)

RW.
BUR.

SINGA-
PORE

TANZANIA

PAPUA
NEW
GUINEA

INDONESIA

ANGOLA
ZAMBIA
MALAWI

VANUATU

FIJI

MOZAM.

NAMIBIA

ZIMBABWE

MADAGASCAR

MAURITIUS

BOTSWANA

RÉUNION

SWAZILAND

AUSTRALIA

LESOTHO

SOUTH
AFRICA

NEW
ZEALAND

Source: Gleick, Peter. *The World's Water 2000–2001.* Island Press, 2000.

Water Tables

Figure 2: The Threat to Groundwater

Industrial and agricultural processes pose a threat to freshwater resources. Without intervention, this threat is cyclical and unending.

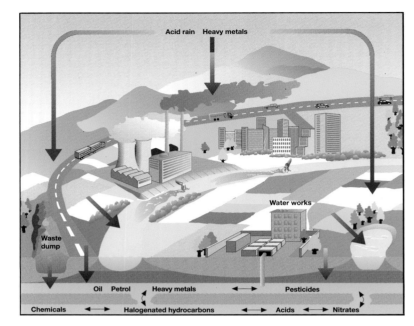

Figure 3: The Water Cycle

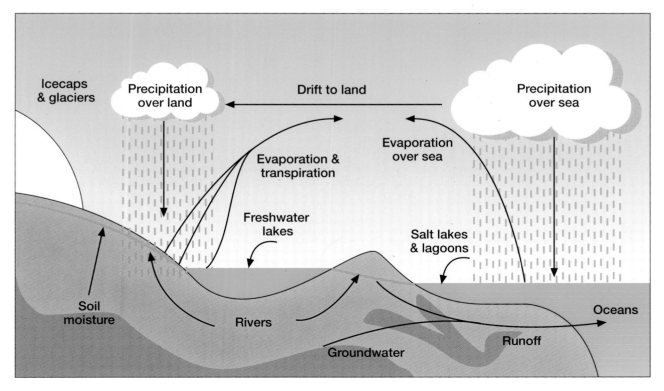

Figure 4: Main Types of Irrigation

	Efficiency
Surface—used in more than 80 percent of irrigated fields worldwide	
Furrow: Traditional method; cheap to install; labor-intensive; high water losses; susceptible to erosion and salinization	20–60%
Basin: Cheap to install and run; needs a large amount of water; susceptible to salinization and waterlogging	50–75%
Aerial (using sprinklers)—used in 10–15 percent of irrigation worldwide	
Costly to install and run; low pressure sprinklers preferable	60–80%
Subsurface ("drip")—used in 1 percent of irrigation worldwide	
High capital costs; sophisticated monitoring; very efficient	75–95%

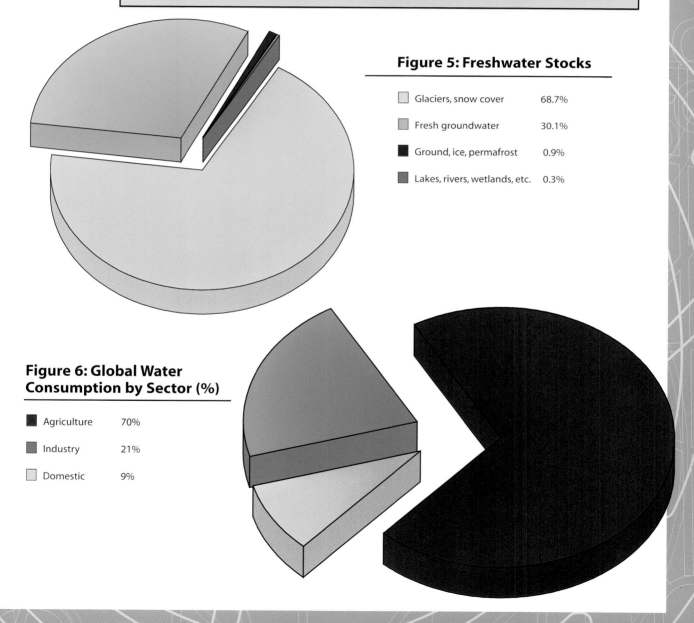

Figure 5: Freshwater Stocks

	Glaciers, snow cover	68.7%
	Fresh groundwater	30.1%
	Ground, ice, permafrost	0.9%
	Lakes, rivers, wetlands, etc.	0.3%

Figure 6: Global Water Consumption by Sector (%)

	Agriculture	70%
	Industry	21%
	Domestic	9%

Using and Conserving Water

In the **developed world**, people have become used to the idea that water is an inexpensive and plentiful resource. The average U.S. citizen, even if he or she lives in a desert region, uses 122 gallons (555 L) of water per day. By contrast, individuals in West Africa survive on less than one gallon (5 L) per day. One-third of the world's population lives on less than 11 gallons (50 L) per day—roughly the amount flushed down the toilet each day by a citizen in the United Kingdom. Water conservation is a necessary step in reducing the strain on our water supply. When countries and their citizens become wealthier, they use more water. More water is being used per person now than ever before. The average citizen in the United States uses approximately 448,000 gallons (1.7 million L) of water per year—4 times the amount used in China and 50 times the amount used in Ethiopia. In the 21st century, a larger global population and an increase in the amount of water used per person will stress the world's limited supply of renewable freshwater. Open-market pricing and conservation are the only ways to resolve this problem in the long term.

Irrigation consumes most of the world's available freshwater. Obviously, improvements in irrigation would make the greatest difference in relieving the strain on our supply of freshwater. At present, we may be wasting as much as half the water used for irrigation. Simple changes could improve the situation substantially, though it is unrealistic to expect very high levels of efficiency in many developing countries. Lack of money, education, skill, and political willpower

Women in developing countries must often haul jugs to provide water for their families.

prevent developing countries from setting up the necessary improvements.

Industry is the second-biggest user of water. Although most industrial use of water is efficient, some industrial processes require vast amounts of water. For example, the production of 2.2 pounds (1 kg) of aluminum may require 330 gallons (1,500 L) of water. Paper production also requires large amounts of water. Though new processes have greatly reduced consumption, there is still plenty of room for big savings in industrial uses of water.

In the rich countries, increases in the price of water, as well as recycling and the use of new technology, have helped to limit or reduce water consumption. In the United States, for example, industry produces four times more than it did in 1950 but uses one-third the amount of water it used

then. Japan and Germany show similar improvements in water use. Japanese industry recycles more than 75 percent of the water used to manufacture goods. However, industrial water consumption is continuing to increase sharply in the developing countries. With domestic and agricultural demands also increasing, the requirements of water supply systems are under growing strain. Many experts believe that the best way to counter

Each day, the average Canadian pulp and paper mill releases about 26,400,000 gallons (100,000,000 L) of toxic wastewater into the environment.

this trend is to impose water charges based on the real cost of supplies. This would motivate consumers to conserve water and recycle the water they use.

Few governments charge realistic prices for water, especially to farmers. Even in California, farmers get water for

WHAT YOU CAN DO TO CONSERVE WATER

There are several ways in which you can reduce the demand for freshwater:

1. Take short showers instead of baths.
2. Turn water off while brushing teeth or washing hands.
3. Convert to low-water toilets.
4. Water the garden during low-evaporation hours (early morning and evening).
5. Choose plants that require less water.

less than one-tenth of its real cost. In many developing countries, there is virtually no charge for irrigation water. In addition, the government pays for most of the cost of energy, too, meaning that farmers can afford to run water pumps day and night. In the United States, where landowners retain rights to water arising on their property, the government has introduced the idea of water trading. Farmers can make money by selling their water to people who live in cities. Water, which was once regarded as free to all, is becoming a commodity that can be bought and sold on the open market.

In the 1970s, increases in the price of oil and concern that supplies were running low led to energy conservation all over the world. People began to invest in new sources of energy. This same spirit of conservation could improve our water use. One way to cut back on water consumption is simply to prevent leaks. It is estimated that in some of the biggest cities of the developing world, more than half of the water entering the system is lost through leaks in pipes, dripping taps, and broken installations. Even in the United Kingdom, water losses were estimated at 25 percent in the 1990s because of poorly maintained pipes.

Huge quantities of water are used in sewage systems, with a typical toilet in Europe flushing away more water in a day than an African family uses in a week

for all domestic purposes. Recent laws in the United States and Japan have required the fitting of 1.3-gallon (6 L) "low-flush" systems to replace the 2.6-gallon (12 L) cisterns that have typically been used in the past. Traditionally, wastewater from sewage pipes, storm drains, and factories has been flushed away and discharged into rivers or the sea. The modern approach, however, views wastewater as a resource that can be put to good use—either in irrigation or, after careful treatment, as recycled domestic water. Israel has spent a significant amount of money on wastewater treatment, recycling as much as 80 percent of its wastewater. Soon, treated wastewater will account for most irrigation water in Israel. A few cities, such as Saint Petersburg, Florida, operate a **closed-loop system**, recycling all municipal wastewater back into domestic systems.

Water conservation may also be achieved through better general management

---

Water conservation may be achieved through better management of the environment.

---

of the environment. Human interference with the ecosystem can have a severe effect on rainfall and water runoff. Forest clearings associated with India's Kabini Dam project reduced

local rainfall by 25 percent. A similar reduction in rainfall has been observed in various other parts of the world where large-scale forest clearance has taken place.

Grass and shrub cover can be just as important in preserving the balance of the water cycle. Land covered in vegetation acts as a sponge that absorbs rainfall. Removal of the vegetation means that rainfall runs off the surface of the land, increasing soil erosion, instead of being gradually fed into the soil to renew groundwater levels.

Global warming may affect rainfall patterns, though controversy surrounds its

■ **Sand and water filters in Orange County, Florida, are designed to treat and recycle sewage water that will be used by farmers to irrigate crops.**

precise effects. As sea levels rise, countries in low-lying coastal areas are likely to be flooded by seawater. Other countries will experience changes in rainfall, which could change the amount of food they are able to grow—either for better or for worse. In broad terms, it is thought that rainfall zones will shift northward, further reducing the amount of water in Africa, the Middle East, and the Mediterranean—a grim prospect indeed.

KEY CONCEPTS

Sustainability Managing the world's water resources is becoming a top global priority. A reliable water supply is essential to support life on Earth. Water supply and demand varies from region to region, but each region faces the common challenge of ensuring water quality and quantity.

Global warming The average temperature on Earth is increasing. Although this may be due in part to natural variation, many scientists believe the increase is largely a result of industrial processes and can ultimately lead to changes in climate. When climate changes, so do patterns of rainfall and sea levels. Climate change can result in a range of impacts on plants and animals.

Clean Water, Dirty Water

During the last 150 years, most of the diseases associated with dirty water have been virtually eliminated from the **mortality** statistics of developed countries. By contrast, in the developing world, about 80 percent of disease is caused by contaminated water.

The United Nations proclaimed 1981–1990 the "Decade of Drinking Water" because the world was concerned about the poor quality of drinking water in the developing countries. Adequate access to safe water might mean a tap within 220 yards (200 m) for city dwellers or one-half mile (1 km) for people in rural areas. During the 1980s, many new local water supplies were established, often incorporating hand-operated pumps. In developing countries, the percentage of the rural population with access to clean drinking water rose from 29 percent to 68 percent during the 1980s, with more than 1 billion people (half of them in China) receiving clean water services for the first time. By 1995, 78 percent of the world's population had access to safe water, but less than half had access to sanitation. As the

Every 15 seconds, a child dies from consuming dirty water.

population grows and people move from rural areas to cities, water facilities in the cities must be improved so that people continue to have access to safe water supplies.

Sanitation systems are almost as important as clean water itself.

Despite the recent advances, many people in developing countries still have to walk long distances to find water and often must share it with many other people. A **standpipe** may serve as many as 1,000 people in some African towns. More than one billion people in the developing world have to rely on whatever water they can get—from rivers, lakes, ditches, shallow wells, and so on. Water from these sources is usually contaminated and can be deadly. In such circumstances, cleanliness and health are almost impossible to maintain. Untreated sewage is the main problem. Adequate sanitation systems are almost as important as clean water itself. The annual cost of water-related disease

FAST FACTS

1. More than 40 percent of U.S. lakes, rivers, and estuaries are too polluted for swimming or fishing.

2. Between 1990 and 1995, corporations were allowed to dump more than 1.5 billion pounds (680 million kg) of toxins directly into U.S. waters.

3. Worldwide, about four million children die each year from diarrheal diseases caused by unsanitary drinking water.

4. Countries that invest in water purification systems can reduce the occurrence of disease by nearly 75 percent.

5. It costs about $3.5 billion per year to operate water systems in the U.S.

6. U.S. residents drink about one billion glasses of tap water each day.

($125 billion per year) is far more than what it would cost to provide clean water and sanitation ($75 billion per year).

Dams and open irrigation channels in tropical areas mean that there are large bodies of still water where mosquitoes (which carry malaria) and other disease-bearing organisms breed. When reservoirs sink to low levels in the summer, even greater swarms of mosquitoes develop. By filling the Akosombo Dam reservoir in West Africa, the infection rate in local children rose from only 10 percent to 90 percent within a single year. Infections from bilharzia (schistosomiasis) increased dramatically in the Nile River Delta as irrigation projects developed after the Aswan Dam was built. Bilharzia parasites cause severe sickness, though rarely death. Diarrhea, often caused by poor hygiene, kills five million people each year. Other common water-related diseases include cholera, typhoid, trachoma, and hookworm. The irony is that water can be made safe to drink through chlorination, ozone, iodine, bleaching powder, or simply by boiling the water to kill bacteria. However, in rural areas, boiling consumes vast amounts of wood fuel, contributing to deforestation.

Water contamination occurs in rich and poor countries alike. Half the population of rich countries can only get clean water from treatment plants because rivers, lakes, and groundwater have been polluted by sewage, fertilizers, pesticides, and industrial chemicals. Heavy metals and chemicals have dissolved in the groundwater and pollute the surface of rivers and lakes. Flowing water can clean itself of these pollutants, but underground aquifers do not flow, and so they are both difficult and expensive to clean up, a process that may take many years. A river may be able to renew itself in two or three weeks, while an aquifer may take hundreds or even thousands of years.

The quality of river water in the developing world is becoming worse all the time.

Most European and American rivers are polluted, but the situation is much better than it used to be. The quality of river water is more closely monitored than ever before. Many rivers and lakes that were once severely polluted with highly toxic chemicals have been restored to health. Unfortunately, the quality of river water in the developing world is becoming worse all the time, with untreated sewage and industrial waste being poured into the rivers at a terrifying rate. About 95 percent of sewage in developing countries is released into rivers without treatment of any kind.

Access to safe drinking water and adequate sanitation are the most important factors for reducing disease and death in the developing world.

WATER-BORNE DISEASES

Water-borne diseases are major causes of death in the developing world. More than one billion people are at risk because they do not have access to clean water.

Bilharzia More than one billion people are at risk of contracting bilharzia. About 300 million people already have the disease. The schistosome parasites develop in snails that live in ponds, streams, and canals. Humans then ingest the parasites, which feed on red blood cells and dissolved nutrients.

Cholera Cholera is caused by an infection in the intestines. Rapid loss of fluids due to diarrhea can cause death within hours.

Cryptosporidiosis A parasite that lives in human and animal intestines causes cryptosporidiosis, a diarrheal disease. The parasite can live for long periods outside the body and is resistant to chlorine. One mouthful of contaminated water can lead to infection.

Dengue Dengue is spread by mosquitoes that breed in stagnant water in artificial containers. More than 1.3 billion people are at risk of contracting this disease, which can cause high fever, joint pain, circulatory problems, and death.

E coli 157:H7 This bacterial strain causes severe diarrhea, bleeding, and cramps. Although E coli is primarily spread through uncooked meat, it can be contracted by swimming in contaminated water.

Giardiasis This is one of the most common water-borne diseases. It is diarrheal and caused by a parasite that lives in the intestines. Giardiasis is contracted through contact with water contaminated with feces.

Hepatitis A This disease can be spread through contact with water contaminated with human feces. Symptoms include fever, loss of appetite, and nausea. Children younger than three years old do not always exhibit symptoms, but they can still spread the virus.

Leptospirosis Water contaminated with the urine of infected animals can spread this bacterial disease. If left untreated, leptospirosis can cause liver damage, meningitis, and death.

Malaria Each year, between 300 million and 500 million people contract malaria. Several million die from it. Unsanitary water bodies provide ideal breeding grounds for the mosquitoes that transmit this disease.

Shigella This bacterial disease causes diarrhea, fever, and stomach cramps. Shigella is spread through contact with fecal matter.

Typhoid Spread by contaminated water, typhoid is common in areas without proper sanitation. If left untreated, typhoid can cause death.

Two billion people living in cities had no access to adequate sanitation in 1999. This number is expected to grow to 3.5 billion by 2025. It will cost $1.8 trillion, or $75 billion per year for the next two decades, to provide all these people with clean water and sanitation. In other words, the total cost to provide clean water, sanitation, and new projects for other water infrastructure—for agriculture and industry, and for renewal of old systems throughout Europe and America—will be $180 billion per year.

Providing water to cities generally requires engineering projects, such as dams, reservoirs, and pipelines. Small rural communities can survive by collecting water in traditional or innovative ways, for example, from wells and dew collection. Because so much of the world's population is shifting to the cities, engineering solutions will be required to provide them with water. When such projects are planned and undertaken, they must be designed so that the impact on the environment and on people is as little as possible. Future projects should be guided by five objectives: fairness to the people who will benefit from the project and to those who will be affected by it; consultation with those people so that the project will fulfill their needs; efficiency of the project, so that water and money are not wasted; sustainability, so that the project will last and cost little to maintain; and accountability, so that those who are responsible for the project will ensure that the job is done in the safest and least expensive way possible.

For billions of people in developing countries, obtaining a day's worth of water means hauling it bucket by bucket.

Duties: Study aquatic ecosystems and advise public or private organizations about water management strategies
Education: Degree in science
Interests: The relationship between living things and the water around them

Navigate to the Environmental Careers Web site: www.eco.org for information on related careers. Also click on www.environmental-jobs.com for more information about jobs for ecologists.

Careers in Focus

An aquatic ecologist studies the relationship between living things and their underwater environment. A major component of an aquatic ecologist's job involves conducting research on water systems.

The day-to-day duties of an aquatic ecologist include a mixture of field research, laboratory experiments, and report writing. He or she will often travel to a water body, collect samples of aquatic plants and animals, and then analyze them and compile a report. Most aquatic ecologists have a science degree. Senior aquatic ecologists usually have a master's degree or a Ph.D. A keen interest in environmental relationships is required to succeed in this field.

Many aquatic biologists begin their careers as ecological research assistants in a university or college, where they perform tasks and conduct research as directed. After a successful term as a research assistant, an aquatic ecologist might then take a position with a government agency or an environmental consulting firm.

Water Wars Ahead?

Will water scarcity lead to war? Has it already? Much of the world's population lives near rivers. Many of these rivers are shared by more than one country. In Europe, for example, 175 international agreements regulate the sharing of water. In other parts of the world, where many countries do not have agreements with their neighbors, no one is certain about who controls or owns the water. When water flows across international borders, the question of which country "owns" the water is difficult to answer. Sometimes, countries reach agreements on how to share water, but when they do not, problems can develop.

The Middle East

There is very little water in the Middle East. Countries such as Libya, Egypt, Israel, Jordan, and Syria compete for the same water supply. These countries already fight over oil, land, and religion, but water shortages could be the worst problem they face. The short supply of water might be the cause of future wars in this part of the world.

Israel has been drawing most of its water from the Jordan River for the past 50 years, but the Jordan passes through Syria before it reaches Israel. When

---

The short supply of water might be the cause of future wars.

Syria started constructing a dam on the Jordan, Israel bombed the construction site and took control of that part of Syria. Israel's largest freshwater reservoir, the Sea of Galilee (Lake Kinneret), is fed by rivers in the Golan Heights, a part of Syria that Israel captured in a war in 1967. In fact, one-third of Israel's freshwater comes from areas Israel captured in the 1967 war.

Those places are still the location of continued fighting between Israel, Syria, and the Palestinians.

In addition, Jewish settlers in the occupied areas are allowed to have far more water at a much lower price than the Palestinians living in neighboring areas. This is just one of the reasons why the Jews and the Palestinians are fighting one another.

Israel and Syria are not the only countries in the Middle East experiencing conflict over water. Syria and Iraq rely on water from the Tigris and Euphrates Rivers, which originate in Turkey. In 1990, when Turkey blocked the Euphrates for a month to fill a reservoir behind the new Atatürk Dam, the water supply in Syria and Iraq slowed to a trickle. Although the new dam in Turkey supplied irrigation water and helped the Kurdish people farm their land, the loss of water to Syria and Iraq caused hardship to the people in those countries.

An aerial view of the Nile River (the thick black line) illustrates its flow. The city on the right is Cairo, Egypt, and the red areas are those covered by vegetation.

FLUID STRATEGIES

Historically, water has played a key role in wars and other conflicts. Even when water has not been a direct cause of tension, water resources have often been targeted.

In 1503, Leonardo da Vinci and Nicolo Machiavelli planned to divert the Arno River, in Italy, away from Pisa during a conflict between Pisa and Florence. The goal was to deprive Pisa of the Arno's water. The plan, however, failed.

The average total supply of water to Middle Eastern countries is less than 1.3 million gallons (4.9 million L) of water per person. Unfortunately, the number of people in those countries is expected to grow by more than half the present number by 2025, meaning that the strain on the water supply will be even greater. How will this affect the people of the Middle East? Will farms be forced out of business because there is too little water to grow food and quench the thirst of a growing population? Will Arabs be forced to import their food because there is not enough water to support farming in those countries?

The Nile

Ten countries share the river basins of the Blue and White Niles in Africa. Under the Nile Water Treaty of 1959, Egypt, the country furthest downstream, gets most of the water from these rivers, but only Sudan and Egypt are bound by the terms of the agreement. Egypt is almost totally dependent on the Nile for its water. Whenever one of the upstream countries wants to build a dam or construct an irrigation project on the Nile, Egypt threatens that country with the possibility of war. For example, Ethiopia, just south of Egypt, desperately needs irrigation water for its farms, as well as a hydroelectric power plant. Egypt will not let Ethiopia interfere with the flow of the Nile, though, for fear that Egypt would be left without the water it needs.

The Aral Sea

In the 1950s, the Soviet Union changed the course of the Amu Darya and the Syr Darya Rivers, which once flowed into the Aral

Engineers discuss a well project in a Cambodian village. Sustainable water projects provide innovative, long-term solutions to the water and sanitation needs of people in developing countries.

per year. This industry supported 60,000 jobs. Now, there are no longer fishermen on the Aral Sea because it is too small to sustain a viable fishing industry. Moreover, wind blows salty, toxic dust off the dry sea bed, endangering the health of thousands of people throughout the region. Meanwhile, cotton is grown in Turkmenistan and Uzbekistan with the help of irrigation water from the Amu Darya and Syr Darya Rivers. It is unlikely that these countries can continue to grow cotton forever as the crop requires more water than irrigation can provide.

India

The sharing of water resources can lead to understanding and cooperation between nations. More than 500 million people live in the valleys of the Indus, Ganges, and Brahmaputra Rivers. This is the largest interconnected irrigation network in the world. Complex water-sharing agreements have

Sea, so that the water would be available for irrigation in Central Asia. The Aral Sea, which was once the fourth-largest inland body of water in the world, has shrunk to one-quarter of its former size and is still shrinking. Before the sea shrank, fishermen supplied the country with 50,000 tons (45,000 t) of freshwater fish

been worked out between India, Pakistan, and Bangladesh.

China

Today, more than 400 Chinese cities are experiencing chronic water shortages. Beijing, Shanghai, and Tianjin each have annual water shortfalls of more than 525 billion gallons (2 trillion L). Water tables are falling by three feet (1 m) a year. So much water has been pumped from northern aquifers that saltwater has invaded the water table. In addition, pollution from sewage and industrial waste is widespread. These factors combined mean that water in 60 percent of the Yellow River area (covering 7,500 miles or 12,000 km of the river and its tributaries) is unfit to drink.

World

Shortages, contamination, and conflicts over water have been occurring for thousands of years. Now, in the 21st century, these issues have reached a critical point. As countries continue to develop, they must do so with the knowledge that water is Earth's most precious resource. It must be respected, conserved, and used wisely. If not, the water crisis might well become the water catastrophe.

KEY CONCEPTS

Cooperation Earth has a limited supply of water. Often, two or more countries find themselves in conflict over this finite resource. When conflict occurs, it can erupt into full-scale war, as it has many times in the past. Strategies of compromise and cooperation are in the best interests of conflicting nations. Through the use of technological advancements and political outreach, water resources can be managed in order to avoid confrontation.

Time Line of Events

7,000 B.C.
Irrigation is practiced along the Nile Valley in Egypt.

6,000 B.C.
Irrigation is widespread in the fertile delta between the Tigris and Euphrates Rivers.

4,000 B.C.
Susa, a city in Iran, pioneers the use of toilets with drainage.

3,000 B.C.
Irrigation is practiced in Pakistan.

2,000 B.C.
China begins to use irrigation.

605–562 B.C.
Residents of Babylon get running water.

400 B.C.
China's Grand Canal is functioning, with more than 1,700 miles (2,700 km) of waterways.

100 B.C.–A.D. 400
Aqueducts carry water throughout the Roman Empire for drinking, bathing, and sanitation.

30 B.C.
Israeli and Hindu cities tend to be sanitary due to strict religious codes regarding cleanliness.

A.D. 80
Rome passes a law to protect water stored during dry periods.

100
Hero of Alexandria experiments with solar-powered pumps.

1153
European monks use the writings of the early Romans to learn about water delivery.

1400
The introduction of force pumps (water wheels) changes the way water is transported. River currents power huge wheels that pump water to reservoirs.

1582
London Bridge gets a waterwheel.

1774
Chlorine is discovered in Sweden.

1852
The South Fork Dam is completed in Pennsylvania.

1898
The colonial powers, Britain and France, come close to war over a conflict regarding the headwaters of the White Nile.

1901
The U.S. creates the first Federal Water Power Act.

1908
Chlorine is used to purify water in a New Jersey reservoir. This is the first U.S. public water supply to be chlorinated in an effort to remove impurities and contaminants.

Some drainage channels built in ancient Greece are still used to channel water during rainstorms.

1928
The St. Francis Dam collapses in California, killing at least 400 people.

1936
The Hoover Dam is completed in Arizona and Nevada.

1940–1945
Hydroelectric dams are singled out as targets during World War II.

1942
Washington State completes construction of the Grand Coulee Dam.

1948
Frank Zybach invents the center-pivot irrigation machine. This development revolutionizes irrigation technology. Zybach receives a patent for his invention two years later.

1972
The U.S. Congress enacts the Federal Water Pollution Control Act.

1974
The Safe Drinking Water Act is passed in the U.S.

1991
The Itaipú Dam is completed in Brazil and Paraguay.

1992
The United Nations lays the framework for World Water Day, to be recognized each year on March 22.

2001
The theme for World Water Day is "Water and Health." The World Health Organization leads the campaign.

Concept Web

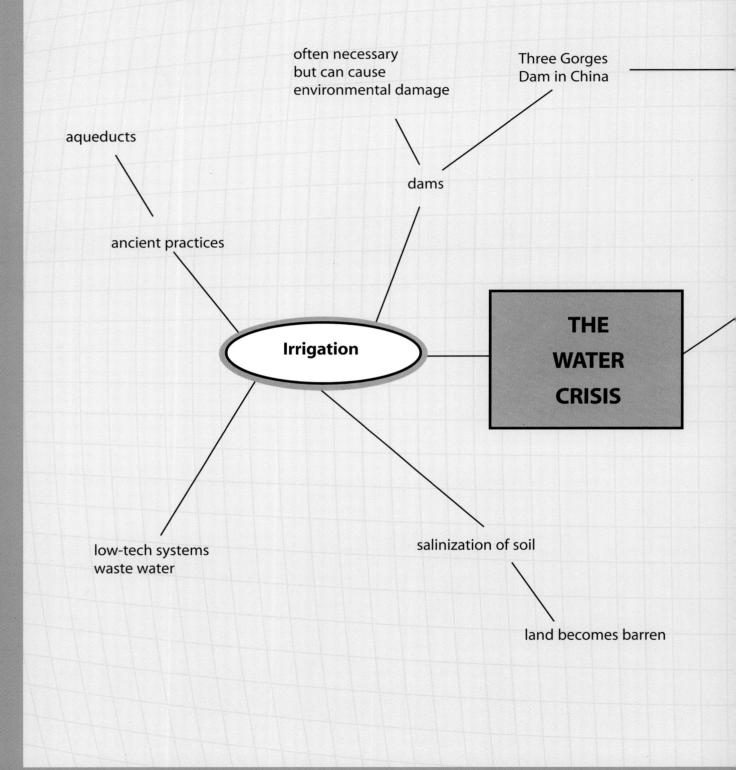

often necessary
but can cause
environmental damage

Three Gorges
Dam in China

aqueducts

ancient practices

dams

Irrigation

**THE
WATER
CRISIS**

low-tech systems
waste water

salinization of soil

land becomes barren

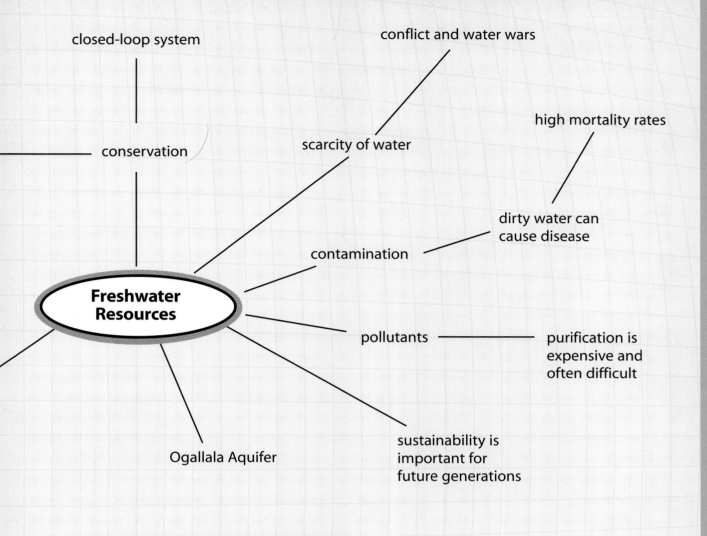

closed-loop system

conflict and water wars

high mortality rates

conservation

scarcity of water

dirty water can cause disease

contamination

Freshwater Resources

pollutants — purification is expensive and often difficult

Ogallala Aquifer

sustainability is important for future generations

MAKE YOUR OWN CONCEPT WEB

A concept map is a useful summary tool. It can also be used to plan your research or help you write an essay or report. To make your own concept map, follow the steps below:

- You will need a large piece of unlined paper and a pencil.
- First, read through your source material, such as *The Water Crisis* in the Understanding Global Issues series.
- Write the main idea, or concept, in large letters in the center of the page.
- On a sheet of lined paper, jot down all words, phrases, or lists that you know are connected with the concept. Try to do this from memory.
- Look at your list. Can you group your words and phrases in certain topics or themes? Connect the different topics with lines to the center, or to other "branches."
- Critique your concept map. Ask questions about the material on your concept map: Does it all make sense? Are all the links shown? Could there be other ways of looking at it? Is anything missing?
- What more do you need to find out? Develop questions for those areas you are still unsure about or where information is missing. Use these questions as a basis for further research.

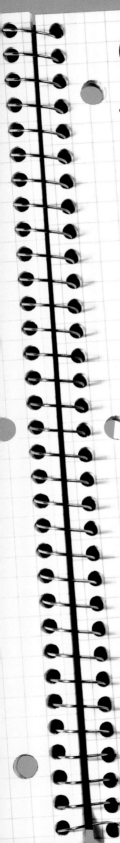

Quiz

True or False

1. About 70 percent of water used worldwide is for irrigation.

2. There is no way to reduce the amount of water people use.

3. More dams are being built in the U.S. today than ever before.

4. Millions of acres of farmland are damaged each year due to waterlogging.

5. One-third of the world's population lives on less than 11 gallons (50 L) of water per day.

6. Cholera, hepatitis A, and shigella are common water-borne diseases.

7. Chlorination is an effective means of water purification.

8. About 70 percent of the world is covered with freshwater.

9. Malaria is seldom fatal.

10. Salinization can be toxic to plants.

Multiple Choice

1. What percentage of the world's population lives in unsanitary conditions?
    a. 10 percent
    b. 20 percent
    c. 30 percent
    d. 40 percent

2. Which country has the most irrigated land?
    a. Singapore
    b. United States
    c. China
    d. Russia

3. Which country was the first to practice large-scale irrigation?
   a. Egypt
   b. China
   c. Iran
   d. Libya

4. What percentage of sewage in developing countries is released into rivers without being treated?
   a. 5 percent
   b. 25 percent
   c. 75 percent
   d. 95 percent

5. How can people reduce the demand for freshwater?
   a. take short showers instead of baths
   b. turn off taps while brushing teeth or washing hands
   c. choose plants that require minimal water
   d. all of the above

6. Which ancient device was invented by a Greek mathematician?
   a. aquifer
   b. pipeline
   c. Archimedes' screw
   d. aqueduct

7. Where is salinization most common?
   a. in areas that receive high amounts of rainfall
   b. in areas that receive low amounts of rainfall
   c. in areas of high elevation
   d. in areas of low elevation

8. Which of the following will become the world's largest hydroelectric plant?
   a. The Three Gorges Dam
   b. The Ogallala Aquifer
   c. The Roman aqueducts
   d. The Hoover Dam

Answers on page 53

Internet Resources

The following Web sites provide additional information about water and conservation:

WATER AND SANITATION PROGRAM

http://www.wsp.org

The Water and Sanitation Program is an international partnership designed to help people gain access to clean water and sanitation services. For two decades, the Water and Sanitation Program has contributed to sustainable solutions for global water services.

INTERNATIONAL WATER ACADEMY

http://www.thewateracademy.org

The International Water Academy seeks to develop water management practices that benefit all people. In partnership with a variety of government, business, and private organizations, the International Water Academy provides educational services regarding the use and conservation of the world's water resources.

U.S. GEOLOGICAL SURVEY

http://www.usgs.gov

The U.S. Geological Survey is an independent fact-finding agency that investigates issues related to the nation's natural resources. Created by an act of Congress, the U.S. Geological Survey has been in operation since 1879.

Some Web sites stay current longer than others. To find other water Web sites, enter terms such as "freshwater," "water conservation," or "salinization" into a search engine.

Further Reading

Beck, Gregor Gipin. *Watersheds*. Willowdale, ON: Firefly Books, 1999.

De Villiers, Marq. *Water*. Toronto, ON: Stoddart, 1999.

Lucas, Eileen. *Water: A Resource in Crisis*. Chicago: Children's Press, 1991.

Postel, Sandra. *Pillar of Sand*. New York: Norton, 1999.

Schnitter, Nicolas. *A History of Dams*. Rotterdam, Netherlands: A. A. Balkema, 1994.

Swanson, Peter. *Water*. Minnetonka, MN: NorthWord Press, 2001.

Woodward, Colin. *Ocean's End*. New York: Basic Books, 2000.

Answers

TRUE OR FALSE:
  1. T 2. F 3. F 4. T 5. T 6. T 7. T 8. F 9. F 10. T

MULTIPLE CHOICE:
  1. d) 2. c) 3. a) 4. d) 5. d) 6. c) 7. b) 8. a)

Glossary

arid: an area with less than 10 inches (25 cm) of rainfall per year

closed-loop system: a system that recycles its own products or waste

developed world: the industrialized countries of the world

developing world: also known as the "Third World," those countries that are less developed economically and technologically than most other nations

divert: to change the route or course (of a river)

estuaries: broad mouths of rivers flowing into the sea, where the river currents meet and are influenced by the sea's tide

Industrial Revolution: the change from an agricultural to an industrial society, which began in England in the mid-18th century

infrastructure: large-scale public systems, services, and facilities

intensive: a system of farming in which large amounts of money and work are spent on a small area in order to maximize production

inundation: the flooding of

levees: embankments designed to prevent the flooding of a river

migration: moving from one region to another

mortality: death rate

optimal: most favorable

pollutants: toxins that contaminate air, water, or soil

porous: having small holes that permit the movement of liquids or gas

salinization: the process of becoming overly salty

standpipe: a large vertical pipe or tower that holds water at a desired pressure

sustain: maintain the existence of

transpiration: the evaporation of water from the surface of plant leaves

Index

Photo Credits